INCUBATING INDONESIA'S YOUNG ENTREPRENEURS
RECOMMENDATIONS FOR IMPROVING DEVELOPMENT PROGRAMS

DECEMBER 2021

ADB

ASIAN DEVELOPMENT BANK

© 2021 Asian Development Bank
6 ADB Avenue, Mandaluyong City, 1550 Metro Manila, Philippines
Tel +63 2 8632 4444; Fax +63 2 8636 2444
www.adb.org

Some rights reserved. Published in 2021.

ISBN 978-92-9269-171-4 (print); 978-92-9269-172-1 (electronic); 978-92-9269-173-8 (ebook)
Publication Stock No. TCS210457-2
DOI: http://dx.doi.org/10.22617/TCS210457-2

The views expressed in this publication are those of the authors and do not necessarily reflect the views and policies of the Asian Development Bank (ADB) or its Board of Governors or the governments they represent.

ADB does not guarantee the accuracy of the data included in this publication and accepts no responsibility for any consequence of their use. The mention of specific companies or products of manufacturers does not imply that they are endorsed or recommended by ADB in preference to others of a similar nature that are not mentioned.

By making any designation of or reference to a particular territory or geographic area, or by using the term "country" in this document, ADB does not intend to make any judgments as to the legal or other status of any territory or area.

Please contact pubsmarketing@adb.org if you have questions or comments with respect to content, or if you wish to obtain copyright permission for your intended use that does not fall within these terms, or for permission to use the ADB logo.

Corrigenda to ADB publications may be found at http://www.adb.org/publications/corrigenda.

Notes:
In this publication, "$" refers to United States dollars.
ADB recognizes "Korea" as the Republic of Korea

Cover design by Josef Ilumin.

Printed on recycled paper

CONTENTS

TABLES, FIGURES, AND BOXES

Tables

Figures

Boxes

ACKNOWLEDGMENTS

Entrepreneurial education has become increasingly important in recent years. As stated by Indonesian President Joko Widodo, the future of Southeast Asia's largest economy lies in the hands of its young entrepreneurs. Entrepreneurship development is a strategic way to harness Indonesia's demographic bonus amid persistently high youth unemployment rates. In line with this, several government ministries provide entrepreneurship training to the youth, including the Ministry of Education, Culture, Research, and Technology (MOECRT), which clearly states in its strategic plan that one of Indonesia's education development objectives is achieving high economic growth supported by sufficient skilled labor with entrepreneurial skills.

The MOECRT has three entrepreneurship development models working toward these objectives: entrepreneurship training programs, incubation centers, and science and techno parks. To support the Indonesian government in this, the Asian Development Bank (ADB), through TA-9678 INO: Supporting the Advanced Knowledge and Skills for Sustainable Growth Project, commissioned a study entitled "Evaluation of Entrepreneurship Development Programs" in 2019–2020. This study aims to draw lessons and good practices from the implementation of incubation centers in three public higher education institutions—the University of Indonesia, Bogor Agriculture University (IPB University), and Politeknik Elektronika Negeri Surabaya (State Electronic Polytechnic of Surabaya) (PENS)—and an entrepreneurship training model facilitated by Swiss–Indonesian start-up accelerator program named Asia Entrepreneurship Training Program (AETP). This report summarizes key findings and offers recommendations for strengthening similar programs in several other universities.

I would like to extend my sincere gratitude to the MOECRT for supporting the study. Special appreciation goes to Gautam Raj Jain and Akbar Fitri of the Inno-Change International Consultants, Inc. of the Philippines who conducted the study, and Jet Damazo-Santos who distilled lessons from the full report into this publication. Contributions from counterparts at the University of Indonesia, IPB University, PENS, and AETP in providing data and information through interviews and focus group discussions are also much appreciated.

Lastly, I would like to thank Rudi Hendrikus Louis Van Dael, ADB senior social sector specialist, who spearheaded the study during his tenure in Indonesia and served as a peer reviewer after he was transferred to the Nepal Resident Mission; Sutarum Wiryono, senior project officer, who supervised the study until its completion; and Maria Angelica Magali Vivar, associate project analyst, who tirelessly handled the administrative and managerial work for the study and publication.

Jakarta, November 2021

Jiro Tominaga
Country Director
ADB Indonesia Resident Mission

ABBREVIATIONS

ADB	Asian Development Bank
AETP	Asia Entrepreneurship Training Program
ANGIN	Angel Investment Network Indonesia
DIIB	Direktorat Inovasi dan Inkubator Bisnis (Directorate of Business Innovation and Incubation)
EDP	entrepreneurship development program
IPB	Institut Pertanian Bogor (Bogor Agricultural Institute)
MOECRT	Ministry of Education, Culture, Research, and Technology
PENS	Politeknik Elektronika Negeri Surabaya (Surabaya State Electronics Polytechnic)
STP	Science and Technology Park
TA	technical assistance
UI	University of Indonesia
US	United States

I. INTRODUCTION

Entrepreneurs Wanted

For Indonesian President Joko Widodo, the future of Southeast Asia's largest economy lies in the hands of its young entrepreneurs.

"They founded start-ups with ideas that could change the world," he said in a speech marking Indonesia's 73rd Independence Day in 2018.[1]

Indonesia is now home to the largest number of unicorn start-ups in Southeast Asia. On-demand transport and logistics service platform GoJek, online marketplaces Tokopedia and Bukalapak, and travel booking platform Traveloka are valued at above $1 billion each. More local start-ups are expected to join their elite circle soon.

Beyond creating jobs and supporting the livelihoods of tens of thousands of micro-entrepreneurs, start-ups are also providing solutions to Indonesia's social problems.

"They established social enterprises which, with noble goals, combine business expertise with a sincere desire to help others," the president said, citing as examples those that employed persons with disabilities and set up waste banks to help protect Indonesia's biodiversity.

"What they are doing has become a source of inspiration for many people, and we must support it. We must pave the way," he said.

For the government, entrepreneurship is also seen to harness Indonesia's demographic bonus amid persistently high rates of youth unemployment. In 2019, the country's 17.04% unemployment rate for youths (aged 15–24 years) was the second highest in Southeast Asia, according to International Labour Organization estimates. It has never strayed far below 15% since the 1997 Asian financial crisis.

With the unprecedented economic disruption caused by the coronavirus disease 2019 (COVID-19) pandemic, the statistics are expected to worsen.

Against this backdrop, it is encouraging to see that more than a third of Indonesian youth say they aspire to become entrepreneurs—a ratio higher than in any other country in the region. In a 2019 survey by the World Economic Forum, 35.5% of youth respondents in Indonesia said they wanted entrepreneurial careers, above

---

[1]   *Antaranews*. 2018. Presiden Sebut Masa Depan Ekonomi Indonesia di Tangan Anak Muda. 16 August. https://bengkulu.antaranews.com/nasional/berita/737748/presiden-sebut-masa-depan-ekonomi-indonesia-di-tangan-anak-muda.

Figure 1: Entrepreneurial Aspirations of Youth in Southeast Asia
(%)

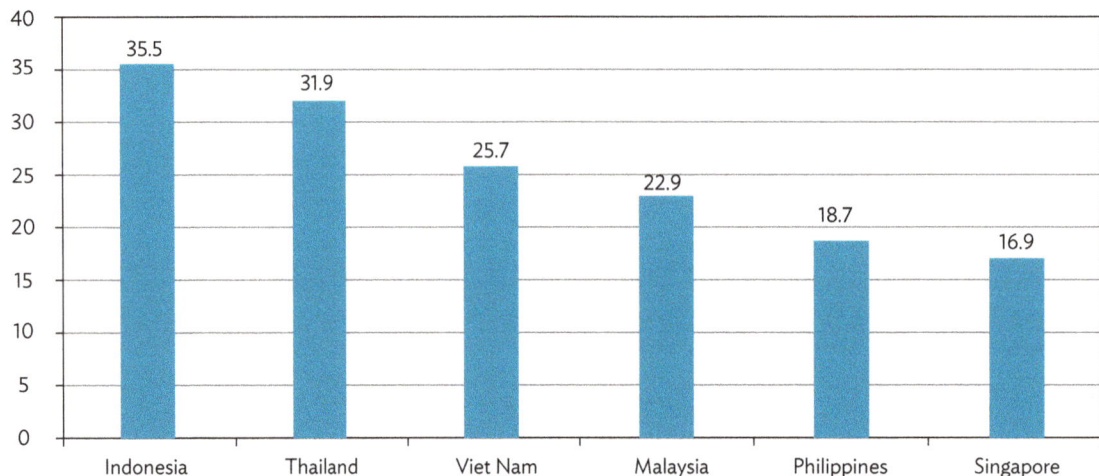

Country	%
Indonesia	35.5
Thailand	31.9
Viet Nam	25.7
Malaysia	22.9
Philippines	18.7
Singapore	16.9

Source: World Economic Forum. 2019. *ASEAN Youth Technology, Skills and the Future of Work*. 16 August. https://www.weforum.org/reports/asean-youth-technology-skills-and-the-future-of-work.

31.9% in Thailand, 25.7% in Viet Nam, 22.9% in Malaysia, 18.7% in the Philippines, and 16.9% in Singapore (Figure 1).[2]

"The extraordinary desire of the Indonesian people to become new entrepreneurs must be empowered to grow and develop," Widodo said.

Entrepreneurship Development Programs: Bridging Aspirations

However, there is a wide gap between wanting to become an entrepreneur and becoming a successful one. One crucial aspect of bridging this gap is ensuring that would-be entrepreneurs are equipped with the knowledge and skills necessary to turn their ideas into sustainable business enterprises.

There are broadly three kinds of entrepreneurship development programs (EDPs) operating in Indonesia today working to bridge this gap:

(a)   incubators run under the support of the government through the Ministry of Education, Culture, Research, and Technology (MOECRT);[3]

---

[2]   World Economic Forum. 2019. *ASEAN Youth Technology, Skills and the Future of Work*. https://www.weforum.org/reports/asean-youth-technology-skills-and-the-future-of-work.

[3]   During the study, the Ministry of Research, Technology and Higher Education managed the incubation programs. In January 2020, the higher education portfolio was added to the Ministry of Education and Culture. In January 2021, the research and innovation component was also given to the Ministry of Education and Culture, and the name of the ministry was changed to Ministry of Education, Culture, Research, and Technology (MOECRT).

(b)   incubators with support from bilateral donors such as the Japan International Cooperation Agency and the Swiss government; and

(c)   incubation centers run by private sector companies through their corporate social responsibility programs.

These programs build on learnings from early approaches, including those initiated by Indonesia's Ministry of Education and Culture. In 2010, the ministry began asking public universities to develop entrepreneurship training programs for students and staff, resulting in about 100 entrepreneurship training centers in various parts of the country.

These early entrepreneurship training centers aimed to develop competencies through 1-day workshops that can be followed by a few credit courses on business skills for more advanced students. They covered topics such as business planning, business policy and strategy, operations management, human resources, marketing, commercial law, communications, and financing. Some of them also offered 6-month practicums involving internships or business incubation.

However, these programs were not comprehensive in their approach, focusing instead on just sensitizing students to the idea of choosing an entrepreneurial path over seeking employment. Given this, the government decided to promote more intensive EDPs, like the business incubators or start-up accelerators that we see today in different parts of the country.

As a comprehensive ecosystem for start-ups, these incubators and accelerators provide a wider range of services to help mitigate the risks that cause so many budding entrepreneurs to fail. Within these programs, in-house entrepreneurs gain not only space to develop their ideas but also mentorship, training, access to information, exhibitions, and networking and funding opportunities. This support can begin even before the actual incubation starts and can extend to years after they exit.

Under the mentorship of academics and industry professionals, participants of these EDPs are encouraged to develop and test their innovative ideas. During the incubation periods that can last from 1–3 years, they are provided with a physical space or coworking space to use. They receive seed capital to produce prototypes and conduct market studies. In addition, they gain guidance on crafting their business strategy and plan. When the students are ready to launch their enterprises, incubators also help them gain access to capital. Universities or professors can even take a stake in the start-ups they mentored.

According to Angel Investment Network Indonesia (ANGIN), the country has seen several start-up assistance organizations like these incubators and accelerators emerge over the past few years, alongside the rise in entrepreneurial interest and activity.[4] Start-ups that have graduated from EDPs have some competitive advantages over those that did not, such as in terms of business models, business management skills, and understanding of financial reporting and accounting.

However, although these EDPs generally have a more comprehensive approach than the training programs that preceded them, their quality still varies from one institution to another, with some able to attract and retain more quality participants than others, and some with better track records of producing successful entrepreneurs.

---

[4]   R. Bhardwaj and C. Ruslim. 2018. *Start-Up Assistance Organizations in Indonesia: Performance, Challenges and Solutions.* ANGIN and Sasakawa Peace Foundation. https://www.spf.org/en/global-data/SAO-Performance-Challenges-Solutions.pdf.

Assessing Indonesian Entrepreneurship Development Programs

Recognizing the contribution of comprehensive EDPs in nurturing start-ups and guiding them along the path toward becoming sustainable enterprises, the MOECRT prepared a medium-term investment plan for higher education aimed at stimulating entrepreneurship at top universities and accelerating innovation in new technology as part of the government's National Medium-Term Development Plan for 2020–2024.

To support this effort, the Asian Development Bank (ADB) financed a study on the Evaluation of Entrepreneurship Development Programs.[5] Aimed at identifying, documenting, and disseminating good entrepreneurship development practices in Indonesia, the study is part of a wider technical assistance (TA) package designed to help strengthen the development of new education programs in the country. The TA also funded an analysis of labor demand and supply trends in the energy sector. All this supports a $200 million project to improve Indonesia's higher education system and upgrade four public universities.

Carried out by Inno-Change International Consultants, Inc. from the Philippines,[6] the study assessed four EDPs selected from a shortlist of 12 candidates to determine what worked and did not work for them. After a preliminary study and visit, the four EDPs were selected based on five parameters: (i) the comprehensiveness of their ecosystems, (ii) the availability of key in-house facilities and services, (iii) the uniqueness of their model, (iv) their access to a supply of innovators such as from undergraduate students, and (v) their learning value.

Each EDP was assessed using surveys and focus group discussions with their tenants and other stakeholders,[7] in addition to quantitative data such as the number of applicants received, acceptance rate, and dropout rate. The study specifically looked at aspects such as how supportive the EDP is for creating and developing new ideas and concepts, whether it can help create a new market for the innovative products developed by start-ups, and how it helps young entrepreneurs gain access to financing and technology. It also looked at the quality of training and mentorship provided, as well as the facilities and business services offered to help reduce start-up difficulties.

The four EDPs studied are briefly profiled below:

IncuBie, IPB University

Founded in 1994, IncuBie (*Pusat Inkubator Bisnis*) is one of the pioneer incubation centers in Indonesia. It was established with the initial aim of commercializing the innovations developed within the state-run Institut Pertanian Bogor (IPB University) (formerly Bogor Agricultural Institute). It is therefore unique for being dedicated to the agriculture sector. Today, it is a fully resourced start-up incubation facility within the IPB campus, just outside Jakarta.

Its tenants are selected through a systematic process and sign onto a 3-year incubation program, during which they gain access to training, mentorship, networking, and finances.

---

[5] The technical assistance (TA)—TA-9678 INO: Supporting the Advanced Knowledge and Skills for Sustainable Growth Project—is funded by a $1.15 million grant from the Japan Fund for Poverty Reduction. This TA is part of the Advanced Knowledge and Skills for Sustainable Growth Project.

[6] The study was led by Gautam Jain and supported by Akbar Fitri. It was supervised by S. Wiryono, senior project officer, ADB Indonesia Resident Mission.

[7] Focus group discussions were conducted for each incubator covering their respective key stakeholders, including members of the management team, collaborators and sponsors, and current and former tenants. See Appendix 1, Table A1.1 for the results of the tenant survey.

Since 1995, it has incubated 265 tenants, 83% of which successfully completed the program and graduated. Of the total, 142 received funding from 25 different agencies. Its tenants have successfully launched well-known innovative products into the Indonesian market, such as healthy food made from Chitosan—sugar from the shells of crustaceans—and an eco-friendly helmet made from palm fruit. One start-up developed cosmetics from spirulina, an herbal breast milk booster from Torbangun leaves, and natural honeybee with various flavors (see Annex B for the lists of IncuBie tenants and services).

Directorate of Business Innovation and Incubation, University of Indonesia

Considered as one of the most successful incubation centers in Indonesia with an impressive 100% success rate in terms of tenants graduating from the program,[8] the Directorate of Business Innovation and Incubation (*Direktorat Inovasi dan Inkubator Bisnis*) (DIIB) was set up in 2015 in response to the needs of the University of Indonesia (UI) students seeking entrepreneurial careers. It was built on the earlier Directorate of Partnership and Business Incubator (*Direktorat Kerjasama dan Inkubator Bisnis*) first established in 2007 by UI and was recently renamed Directorate of Science and Techno Park (*Direktorat Science dan Techno Park*).

Open only to UI students or alumni, DIIB's incubation program runs for 1 year following 6 months of pre-incubation support that includes training and preparing applicants for pitching and participation in exhibitions. Most of its tenants are expected to graduate after a year, although 1-year extensions may be granted as needed. Tenants may also apply for post-incubation acceleration of their enterprises after graduation, where DIIB can offer support in networking with the government.

Of the 91 tenants it has incubated since 2015, about a third have won prestigious awards locally and internationally for their innovations, contributing to DIIB's reputation as a successful incubator. DIIB itself has received recognition, including the Technology Business Incubator Award for the incubation of the Technology-Based Starter Company from the Ministry of Research, Technology and Higher Education in 2018, and the Presidential Award from the International Council for Small Business Indonesia in 2019 (see Annex D for the lists of DIIB tenants and services).

PENS Sky Venture, Surabaya State Electronics Polytechnic

PENS Sky Venture is a center of excellence within the Politeknik Elektronika Negeri Surabaya (Surabaya State Electronics Polytechnic) (PENS), a polytechnic center known for breakthrough electronic innovations, including in robotics. Initially established to cater to its students and commercialize the research-based innovations of its academic community, it now hosts an increasing number of tenants selected and sponsored by MOECRT.

Its incubation process runs for 3 years. However, for tenants supported and selected by MOECRT, incubation is initially offered for 1 year, with the possibility of extension for another 2 years if they have good potential.

PENS Sky has struggled to attract applicants from within PENS and has had fewer tenants than the other incubators assessed by the study. However, many of its graduates have posted impressive rates of return, ranging from 30% to as high as 72%. It has also hosted start-ups with a wide range of innovative products such as a portable underwater robot, soybean breaking and yeast mixing machines, and an online psychologist service (see Annex C for the lists of PENS Sky tenants and services).

---

[8]   Success rate here refers to how many of an incubator's accepted tenants complete its program and graduate from it. In some incubators, tenants may drop out from the program due to various reasons such as inability to produce a viable product.

Asia Entrepreneurship Training Program

The Asia Entrepreneurship Training Program (AETP) is a Swiss–Indonesian start-up accelerator program launched in March 2019 to open the European market for Indonesian start-ups and, conversely, the Asian market for Swiss start-ups. Unlike the incubation programs, the AETP targets advanced ventures with viable products that want to expand internationally.

Supported by the Swiss government under the mandate of Leading House Asia of ETH Zurich in collaboration with the ZHAW School of Management and Law, the free program offered a 5-day training course delivered over 9 months as well as mentorship, and then culminated in visits to Switzerland and Indonesia to access investors. At the time of the study, however, the program was still under implementation, so a conclusive assessment was not possible (see Annex E for the lists of PENS Sky tenants and services).

II. RECOMMENDATIONS

Based on the qualitative and quantitative assessments carried out and the comprehensive case studies developed on these EDPs, the study came up with some recommendations (Table 1).

Most of the recommendations are aimed at the incubators themselves, categorized based on whether they relate to institutional capacity, the services they offer, and how they can continue improving in the future. Some of the recommendations, though, cannot be implemented by incubators alone and would need the support of the universities that operate them or the government through MOECRT.

Table 1: Summary of Recommendations

A. Institutional Capacity

i. Management and Human Resources

- Universities should establish a strong supervisory or advisory board for their incubators. This board should comprise diverse expertise, leveraging the resources of the university when possible.
- Universities and incubators should cultivate a dedicated and experienced management team with a sufficient staff-to-client ratio.

ii. Financial Sustainability

- Incubators should diversify funding sources to reduce overreliance on funding from their parent institution or the government.
- Incubators should work toward self-sustainability by ensuring funding sources increasingly include revenue from rent and service fees.

B. Start-Up Services Offered

i. Pre-Incubation/Acceleration Phase

- Incubators should study the target market to determine concerns and motivations for pursuing a career in entrepreneurship.
- Incubators should improve marketing and communications to raise awareness, build trust, and attract the right applicants.
- Incubators should provide initial training and coaching to prepare applicants for pitching their concepts.

ii. Access to Mentorship and Training

- Incubators should expand their roster of mentors to sufficiently cater to all tenants, including both technical and business development needs.
- Incubators should work with both the public and private sectors to develop a network of experts across Indonesia that could be tapped as mentors as needed.
- Incubators should ensure mentorship and training programs support offbeat ideas and include consumer behavior research and the creation of demand for new products and services.
- Incubators should ensure mentorship and training programs are needs-based and consider the unique needs of targeted start-ups.

continued on next page

Table 1 continued

iii. Access to Business Services and Facilities
- Incubators should ensure sufficient office space and infrastructure to support the development of products and services.
- Incubators should provide business services such as business registration, permits and licenses, etc.

iv. Access to Funding
- Incubators should provide guidance on how to prepare winning investment proposals.
- Incubators should provide guidance on how to use funding grants efficiently.

v. Graduation and Post-Incubation
- Incubators should establish clear exit criteria for graduation, including readiness to implement growth plans.
- Incubators should provide post-incubation services such as access to specialized facilities as needed, consulting services, CEO roundtables, and networking functions.

C. Institutional Improvements

i. Documentation and Evaluation
- Incubators should keep track of graduates and collect data on performance.
- Incubators should analyze collected data regularly to use as a basis for evaluating incubation services and programs.

ii. Developing a Strong Network
- Incubators should develop and leverage a strong network within academic and business communities, as well as with government agencies and state-owned enterprises, to create a strong ecosystem. Accomplishing this will require the support and participation of their parent institutions and the government through MOECRT.

CEO = chief executive officer, MOECRT = Ministry of Education, Culture, Research, and Technology.

Source: Asian Development Bank (ADB). 2019. TA 9678-INO: Evaluation of Entrepreneurship Development Program, Final Report. Unpublished.

Institutional Capacity

Management and Human Resources

As is the case in any institution or organization, the quality of the incubators studied varied in line with the type of management structure and human resources devoted to them. But according to a research study that drew out best practices from 111 successful incubators in the United States (US) in 2011, management is not only an important element to EDP success, it is also one of the factors that matter most.[9]

Specifically, the US study said best practices related to the composition of advisory boards and the hiring of qualified staff that spend sufficient time with clients are among those that result in more successful incubation programs, clients, and graduates.

Recommendations for Universities and Incubators
- Establish a strong supervisory or advisory board for their incubators. This should comprise diverse expertise, leveraging the resources of the university when possible.
- Cultivate a dedicated and experienced management team with sufficient staff-to-client ratio.

This was evident among the Indonesian EDPs studied. IncuBie, for example, benefits from being managed by a dedicated team comprising professionals with specializations in key areas ranging from livestock and post-harvest technology to economics, finance, and marketing (Figure 2). The center's seven full-time staff members, headed by a director specializing in agriculture engineering, have 9 to 14 years of work experience in technology business incubation.

---

[9]   D.A. Lewis, E. Harper-Anderson, and L.A. Molnar. 2011. *Incubating Success: Incubation Best Practices That Lead to Successful New Ventures.* University of Michigan. https://www.academia.edu/20793467/Incubating_Success_Incubation_Best_Practices_that_Lead_to_Successful _New_Ventures.

Figure 2: Management Structure of IncuBie

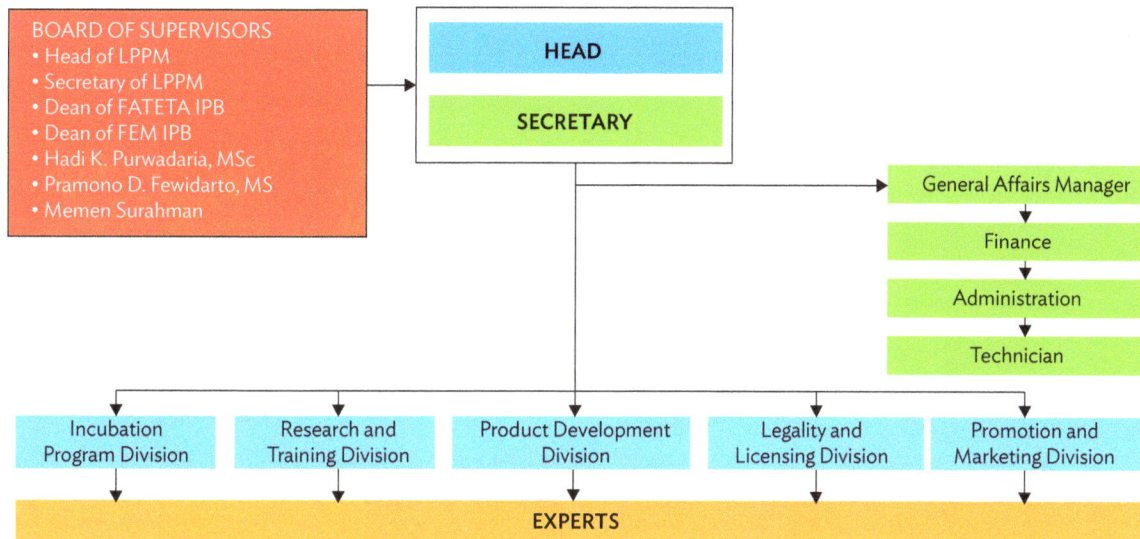

BOARD OF SUPERVISORS
- Head of LPPM
- Secretary of LPPM
- Dean of FATETA IPB
- Dean of FEM IPB
- Hadi K. Purwadaria, MSc
- Pramono D. Fewidarto, MS
- Memen Surahman

HEAD

SECRETARY

General Affairs Manager

Finance

Administration

Technician

| Incubation Program Division | Research and Training Division | Product Development Division | Legality and Licensing Division | Promotion and Marketing Division |

EXPERTS

FATETA = Fakultas Teknologi Pertanian, FEM = Fakultas Ekonomi dan Manajemen, IPB = Institut Pertanian Bogor, LPPM = Lembaga Pengabdian Pada Masyarakat,

Source: ADB. 2019. TA 9678-INO: Evaluation of Entrepreneurship Development Program, Final Report. Unpublished.

Diverse expertise is important, according to the US study, as it can help develop quality business assistance services, embed the EDP in the broader community, market the incubator, and provide effective program oversight. The study also recommended having an experienced entrepreneur, a business lawyer, and a chamber of commerce representative, among others.

Beyond expertise, IncuBie's management team was also lauded by its tenants for creating a family environment at the incubation center. The staff help tenants prepare milestone-based plans as soon as they are inducted, and then follow up rigorously to ensure progress. The management team, trainers, and mentors understood tenants' problems and were committed to supporting and guiding them.

While DIIB also had full-time staff managing its program (Figure 3), the 6-member team comprising an incubation manager and 5 assistant managers (to oversee selection, training, evaluation, exhibition, and networking) was not enough to manage the large and complex activities of the 33 tenants it has at any given time.

According to the US study, high staff-to-client ratios were strongly correlated to client firm performance, and DIIB's 6:33 staff-to-client ratio fares poorly compared with IncuBie's 7:20 ratio.

Consequently, it was a challenge for the DIIB management team to implement all their plans according to schedule, with delays in providing support services due to complex coordination. This led to tenants failing to achieve certain targets, which then affected the evaluation of their progress.

High attrition and the annual rotation of other DIIB staff also caused disruptions and meant that not everyone on the team is familiar with the ongoing work. DIIB should therefore prepare a guidebook on the implementation of its services to maintain consistent quality and timely delivery.

Figure 3: Management Structure of the Directorate of Business Innovation and Incubation

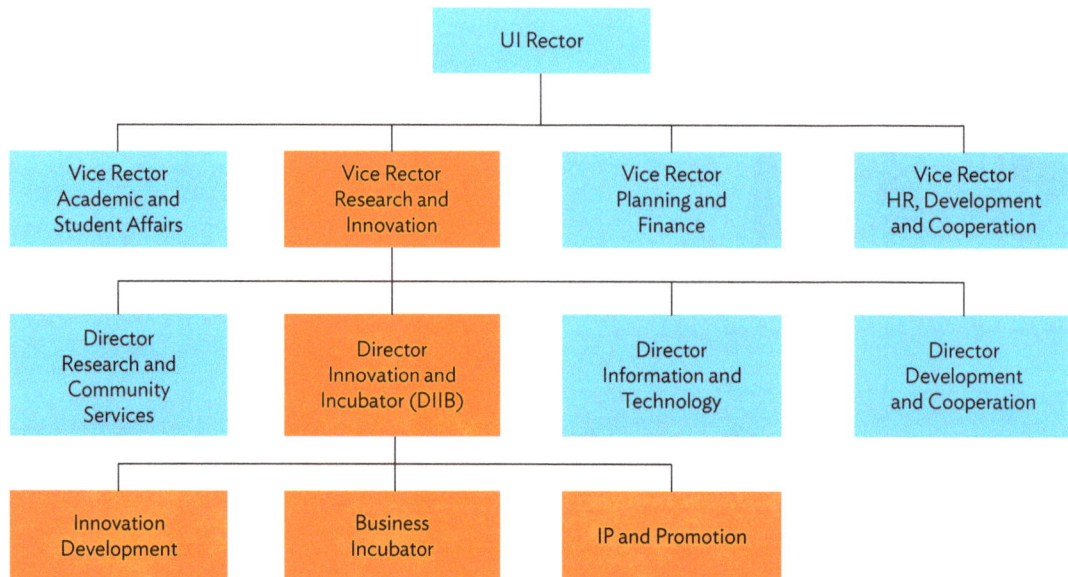

```
                              UI Rector
                                 |
    ┌────────────────┬───────────┴───────────┬────────────────┐
Vice Rector      Vice Rector           Vice Rector        Vice Rector
Academic and     Research and          Planning and       HR, Development
Student Affairs  Innovation            Finance            and Cooperation
    |                |                     |                  |
Director         Director              Director           Director
Research and     Innovation and        Information and    Development
Community        Incubator (DIIB)      Technology         and Cooperation
Services             |
            ┌────────┼────────┐
        Innovation  Business  IP and Promotion
        Development Incubator
```

IP = intellectual property, HR = human resources, UI = University of Indonesia.
Source: ADB. 2019. TA 9678-INO: Evaluation of Entrepreneurship Development Program, Final Report. Unpublished.

However, DIIB benefits from strong leadership and commitment from UI, which are important factors behind its growth and success. This was evident in the vision and commitment of the top management to become self-sustaining through direct funding, as well as the establishment of a vast partnership network. Its three-layer organizational structure is headed by the rector, who oversees the DIIB's operations on behalf of the university through the vice rector for research and innovation.

The importance of strong leadership and dedicated full-time staff is made even more evident when looking at the difficulties encountered by PENS Sky Venture. Although the Surabaya-based incubator is headed by a representative from PENS who oversees its activities and plans, the head exercises limited responsibility for their execution.

Instead, its incubation manager oversees everything from administrative matters to coordinating with sponsors, PENS, and tenants. Though the manager is supported by three assistants—one each for pre-incubation, incubation, and post-incubation—they have limited roles in practice (Figure 4).

PENS Sky's overdependence on the incubation manager not only creates risks in case the manager cannot work but also slows down operations as no other person can make decisions and provide administrative guidance. Consequently, activities are not always implemented as planned, resulting in some tenants dropping out. The lack of autonomy at the operations level also restricts the center's ability to accommodate the changing and unique needs of innovators and start-ups.

Reviewing and revamping PEN Sky's management and organizational structure to better integrate it with the PENS academic community could help address these weaknesses. By involving key PENS faculty members in

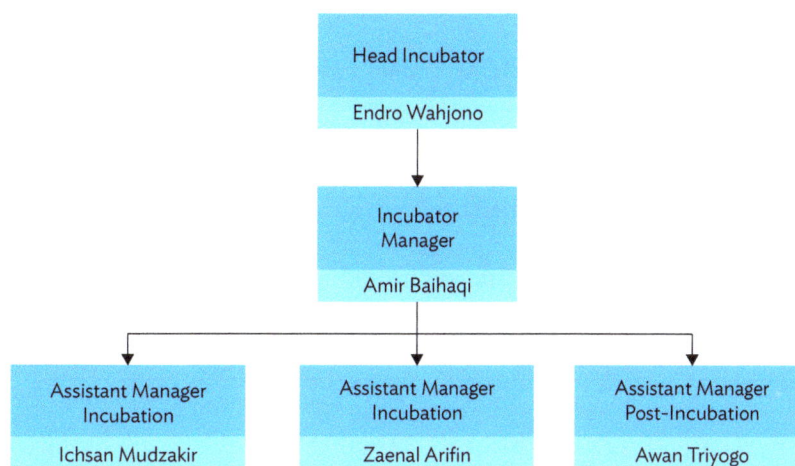

Figure 4: Management Structure of PEN Sky Venture

Source: ADB. 2019. TA 9678-INO: Evaluation of Entrepreneurship Development Program, Final Report. Unpublished.

leadership positions within PENS SKY management, the center could benefit from a wider range of expertise and connections.

Unlike the three other incubators, which are well-established organizations within educational institutions, AETP is a 1-year project managed by a temporary project team that consisted of one manager and selected mentors from both countries.

Financial Sustainability

It would not surprise anyone to learn that, as international studies have found, incubation programs with larger budgets typically outperform those with budget constraints (footnote 9). But where should this budget come from, and what kind of funding model works best for EDPs?

The same international studies show that most successful incubators are not-for-profit organizations but are nonetheless self-sustaining. To reduce dependency on funding sources, they generate income from fees charged to tenants, as well as equity participation in the start-ups or royalty payments.

Recommendations for Incubators
- Diversify funding sources to reduce overreliance on funding from parent institution or the government.
- Work toward self-sustainability by ensuring funding sources increasingly include revenue from rent and service fees.

While all the Indonesian EDPs studied have not-for-profit models, most rely heavily on internal funding from their respective universities and government support, with varied results. Some also attempt to generate revenue through fees and royalties but with far more limited success.

Overreliance on Funding

DIIB, being fully funded by UI, is the least dependent on external and other sources of funds among the four EDPs. UI has committed to meet the cost of the incubation center's operations, covering the tenants' offices, salaries, and other overhead expenses. This support is sufficient to allow the incubator not to charge its tenants for the use of its facilities. While it also receives grants from external sources, it can mostly cover its operational costs through the university's financial support.

PENS Sky Venture is similarly financially dependent on PENS, which covers expenses such as salaries, utilities, and training, and provides the building, furniture, and equipment the incubator uses. This financial support allows it to offer its incubation services to tenants for free. It does not require its tenants to agree to any equity participation or profit-sharing arrangements either. The polytechnic also provides technical and business mentors for the incubator's tenants as needed. Faculty members even volunteer as and when requested.

In addition, PENS Sky Venture receives funding support from MOECRT for the cost of incubation of the tenants it recommends and sponsors. This support includes salary for mentors as well as transportation for mentors, tenants, and facilitators. In addition, MOECRT also shares 25% of the total grant provided to each tenant with PENS Sky Venture for meeting the cost of incubation activities and other overheads.

However, PENS Sky Venture's reliance on just PENS and MOECRT for funding has meant that it has to adjust its expenses to fit the budget, which is often allocated to meet its needs just for each year. This means that it usually does not have funds for future expansion and capacity building in terms of technical, technological, and business management needs. The incubation center also only has a workspace for 10 tenants, which is quite limited as the demand for incubation from PENS' graduates and students is much higher.

IncuBie also relies on IPB for key resources such as land and building, technology and production infrastructure, mentorship from faculty members, and funds for operational expenses. But the incubator realized early on that sustaining its operations meant exploring new sources of funding.

IncuBie head Deva Primadia, who joined the program as a full-time manager in 2001, submitted over 20 proposals to public and private organizations in a year, resulting in the government allocating a budget line for incubation centers that meet key performance indicators based on tenants and successful start-ups. About 15% of the incubator's budget is now financed by sponsorships and other forms of partnerships with various institutions.

Generating Revenue

Ideally, according to a study from Thailand, incubation centers should sustain themselves by generating income from tenants to reduce their dependence on funding. Aside from charging fees during the incubation, they can explore equity participation or royalty arrangements with tenants as revenue sources.[10]

Among the Indonesian EDPs assessed, only IncuBie generates revenue to help sustain its operations. About 20% of its costs are covered by rental fees from tenants and another 15% from industrial and laboratory analysis services. If it can increase the contribution of these revenue sources to its budget, the more sustainable and independent it can be.

On average, according to the US study, nearly 60% of an incubator's budget is accounted for by rent and service fees (footnote 10). Incubators receiving a larger portion of their revenue from rent and service fees performed better than other programs (Table 2).

[10]   S. Yamockul, R. Pichyangkura, and A. Chandrachai. 2019. University Business Incubators: Best Practice Factors Affecting Thailand UBI Performance. *Academy of Entrepreneurship Journal*. 25 (1). https://www.abacademies.org/articles/university-business-incubators-best-practice-factors-affecting-thailand-ubi-performance-7836.html.

As indicated in Table 2, IncuBie also expects to generate revenue from royalty payments. Each tenant's contract contains a provision for the payment of royalties upon graduation or after 3 years. However, it has yet to receive any, as it does not have a system to track the financial performance of the start-ups that have graduated from it.

To address this issue, incubators and tenants should develop a 5-year projection of revenue and expenses before graduation, which will be used as the basis of royalty payments later. This projection may subsequently be adjusted based on audited financial figures.

For a start-up company to grow, finding the right partner is crucial. The incubator could help tenants expand their network and explore potential collaboration for the product and market development. Box 1 illustrates how a tenant successfully developed collaboration with partners at DIIB UI.

Table 2: IncuBie Revenue Stream (%)

Sources of Revenue	Contribution
Indonesian government budget from the Ministry of Research, Technology and Higher Education	50
Rental/profit sharing from STP IPB	20
Industrial services	10
Partnerships with other institutions	10
Laboratory analysis services	5
Sponsorships	5
Royalty/profit sharing from successful tenants	0

STP IPB = Science and Techno Park IPB University.
Source: ADB. 2019. TA 9678-INO: Evaluation of Entrepreneurship Development Program, Final Report. Unpublished.

Box 1: ATM Sehat: Finding Partners for a Healthy Business

Sigit Nuzul knows firsthand how difficult it is to turn an innovative idea into a real business, especially with a goal as ambitious as creating a device that can provide remote medical services in poor rural areas across Indonesia.

In 2016, he began working on a telehealth tool when he was still a nursing student at the University of Indonesia (UI). He was lucky, as the university is home to a network of supportive faculty members as well as one of the best incubators in the country, the Directorate of Business Innovation and Incubation (DIIB).

He found a partner in Ahmad Zaki Anshori from UI's Faculty of Computer Science. They took part in a student creativity program by the Ministry of Research, Technology and Higher Education. Their proposal was funded and they were given the opportunity to participate in an expo.

"After this event, I immediately registered this telehealth tool to get a patent," he said.

After they officially joined DIIB as a tenant in 2017, he invited Budhi Mulyadi, who at that time was taking his doctorate degree at the Faculty of Nursing, to join the telehealth team.

"He gave a lot of valuable input to the team, especially those related to emergency function tools, which at the time had panic button features," Sigit said.

They soon began working on producing the prototype for ATM Sehat device but encountered problems in finding a company to manufacture it. The main hurdle was related to government regulations on the production of medical devices.

"Initially, we could not get a suitable partner because we did not have permission to produce medical devices. But in the end, through the network of our supervisor Taufik Jamaan, we finally partnered with a state-owned medical device producer," he said.

continued on next page

Box 1 continued

ATM Sehat is now being trialed in some urban poor and rural areas, allowing users to check several health indicators such as blood pressure, blood sugar, cholesterol, weight and height, temperature, blood oxygen levels, and lung capacity. The results are stored in an ATM Sehat application on a smartphone.

Through an ATM Sehat, users can also consult with a health worker to get help in interpreting the results of the health checks, get in-depth education about illnesses and how to prevent complications, and get a referral to a health facility in case they need treatment. It even has a panic button to call an ambulance or a health worker in case of emergencies.

Through an integrated access to an online pharmacy, users can also purchase supplements and other health products and have them delivered to their home. Users can even register for or check the status of their insurance through an ATM Sehat.

Since the ATM Sehat is designed for remote and disadvantaged communities, it is equipped with solar panels to provide electricity and satellite internet for connectivity—a solution also achieved through a partnership.

"At first, this device was not equipped with solar panels and satellite internet until I met Tomy Abuzairi from the Faculty of Engineering. He helped us make an ATM Sehat prototype that could be used in remote areas using solar panels and satellite internet," he said, adding that they even managed to create a portable version powered by solar electricity.

The company has since received various awards and recognition, such as being included in a book on 109 Indonesian Innovations in 2017 and winning an ASEAN-level information technology innovation competition in the Lao People's Democratic Republic.

"Through this competition, we not only gained prestige but also expanded our partnerships and the ATM Sehat network to various stakeholders, including relevant ministries," he said.

"If we discuss ideas by collaborating with others, there will be many additions and inputs that will perfect the idea. And we will definitely get partners who have the same vision and are willing to try hard to make that idea a reality."

Source: ADB. 2019. TA 9678-INO: Evaluation of Entrepreneurship Development Program, Final Report. Unpublished.

Start-Up Services

Pre-Incubation/Acceleration Phase

Before any incubation or acceleration services can be provided, EDPs first have to surmount the initial hurdle of attracting quality start-ups to apply and join. Beyond just selecting tenants, this crucial stage involves not only inspiring new entrepreneurs and marketing your services effectively but also involving ideally a combination of training and business planning, market research, and milestone setting before final selections are made.

Encouraging Entrepreneurship

PENS Sky Venture has a comprehensive three-level pre-incubation process that PENS students and alumni go through.

In the first level, PENS students are encouraged to participate in creativity programs, where they are guided and supported in developing innovative products. In the second level, they are required to complete this project as a requirement for graduation. This is designed to motivate them to become entrepreneurs rather than seek employment, and to sensitize them to incubation at a later stage.

In the third level, PENS graduates are invited to pursue their interest in entrepreneurship by using the PENS technical workshop facility to develop innovative products. These graduates can later apply to join PENS Sky Venture to pursue their business plans. This pre-incubation period can last for 1 year, during which they receive coaching and mentoring. Participants also have to showcase their product technology and pitch for incubation.

Despite this comprehensive approach, however, PENS' pre-incubation activities have not been effective in motivating PENS students to consider entrepreneurial careers and join PENS Sky Venture.

Recommendations for Incubators
- Study the target market to determine concerns and motivations for pursuing a career in entrepreneurship.
- Improve marketing and communications to raise awareness, build trust, and attract the right applicants.
- Provide initial training and coaching to prepare applicants for pitching their concepts.

Table 3 shows that only a few start-ups apply for incubation at PENS Sky Venture and that even fewer come from within PENS. Based on the ratio of the number of its applicants to the number of tenants, it is evident there was hardly any selection needed, as most applicants end up being offered admission. Most of the incubator's tenants now come in through MOECRT's own review and selection process.

Table 3: PENS Sky Venture Applicants and Tenants

Data on Tenants	2016	2017	2018	2019	Total
No. of applications	1	10	8	13	32
No. of tenants accepted	1	8	6	11	26
No. of tenants supported by MOECRT	1	8	5	11	25
No. of tenants not supported by MOECRT	0	0	1	0	1
No. of tenants from PENS	1	7	3	3	14
No. of tenants not from PENS	0	1	3	8	12

MOECRT = Ministry of Education, Culture, Research, and Technology; PENS = Politeknik Elektronika Negeri Surabaya.
Source: ADB. 2019. TA 9678-INO: Evaluation of Entrepreneurship Development Program, Final Report. Unpublished.

Research indicates that PENS students still prefer the security of regular employment to a riskier entrepreneurial career. Therefore, a survey of PENS' students should be conducted to find out the key factors associated with their decisions or motivations to be an entrepreneur. Accordingly, a new policy for attracting internal students should be formulated to strengthen the pre-incubation program.

Communicating Effectively

Even among those already inclined to become entrepreneurs, joining an EDP is still not a common option. In a survey by Angel Investment Network Indonesia (ANGIN),[11] 55% of start-up owners said they did not apply to any incubator or accelerator. The top reason was the competitive selection process involved and the lack of an accessible program in their region. But interestingly, some start-ups also said they were not aware of EDPs, or they were aware but did not see any benefits from joining them, or they had been told joining one was not recommended.

---

[11]   R. Bhardwaj and C. Ruslim. 2018. *Start-Up Assistance Organizations in Indonesia: Performance, Challenges and Solutions.* ANGIN. https://www.spf.org/en/global-data/SAO-Performance-Challenges-Solutions.pdf.

This problem indicates that EDPs have an awareness and reputational issue to address. It is important for programs to clearly communicate what they are looking for and offering to attract the right applicants. This was seen in the experience of AETP, which was an accelerator targeting advanced start-ups in Indonesia and Switzerland that were ready to expand internationally with developed prototypes, and not an incubator for budding business ideas.

To attract the interest of potential innovators, the AETP team conducted several roadshows in three key cities —Jakarta, Yogyakarta, and Malang—to recruit start-ups that were appropriate for the program. Specifically, they were looking for Indonesian enterprises with disruptive concepts that had already gone past the seed stage and wanted to expand internationally. This means the start-ups should already have ready prototypes and have achieved market validation for profit.

The communications materials used, however, emphasized the admission criteria—specifically the part about having a ready prototype—and did not clearly state that the program is for those who wish to enter the Swiss market. As a result, most of the 150 applications from across Indonesia sought support for operational launch within the country and were far from ready to expand internationally. Out of the 150 applications, 30 start-ups were shortlisted and 10 were accepted. But of the 10, half eventually dropped out.

On the Switzerland side, the AETP campaign to seek applicants promoted largely the same criteria for admission. However, a key difference was that their communications materials clearly stated they were looking for entrepreneurs who wanted to expand and enter the Indonesian market, consequently generating interest from more appropriate enterprises. The campaign resulted in 25 applications, out of which four were selected.

As with PENS Sky Venture, AETP's challenges stemmed from an incomplete understanding of its target market's needs. One of the main issues with the program was that it was conceptualized based on the understanding of incubation and accelerators in Switzerland and had a limited understanding of Indonesian culture and its start-up ecosystem.

Comprehensive Preparation

Among the EDPs surveyed, the pre-incubation program of UI's DIIB stood out for getting a 100% intake of tenants from the university's students and for being able to leverage the research outputs of its faculty members (Table 4).

Table 4: Directorate of Business Innovation and Incubation Applicants and Tenants

Data on Tenants	2015	2016	2017	2018	2019	Total
No. of applications	N/A	57	67	103	94	321
No. of tenants accepted	7	15	21	22	33	98
No. of tenants supported by MOECRT	3	1	8	3	7	22
No. of tenants from UI	7	15	21	22	33	98
No. of start-up graduated	7	15	21	22	33	98

N/A = not applicable, MOECRT = Ministry of Education, Culture, Research, and Technology; UI = University of Indonesia.

Source: ADB. 2019. TA 9678-INO: Evaluation of Entrepreneurship Development Program, Final Report. Unpublished.

In DIIB, the pre-incubation phase is largely about preparing students, who are already interested in entrepreneurship, to pitch to be selected as tenants. It starts with a call for applications sent out to UI students and graduates. The applicants then undergo a program of socialization into the incubation environment. They are also invited to participate in the UI Preneur Camp, a 3-day workshop participated by 50 UI students with their respective teams, where different speakers from partner institutions provide coaching.

Overall, the pre-incubation process involves up to 6 months of preparatory grooming involving workshops, training, mentoring, and opportunities for exhibition as well as business matching sessions. This also enables those not selected to join the actual incubation program to still pursue their business ideas, having benefitted from 6 months of learning and grooming.

Access to Mentorship and Training

Mentorship and training are not only sought-after services from EDPs but are also key factors in the success of incubated start-ups.

In a survey of participants of start-up assistance organizations by ANGIN, 79% said they were seeking mentors when they joined the incubation programs (footnote 11). The 2011 US study on incubators also found strong mentor programs to be statistically significantly related to client firm performance.

However, Indonesian EDPs do not have a strong track record when it comes to providing mentoring services. In the same ANGIN survey, 94% of participants said the mentors in their program did not have relevant technical experience, 76% said their mentors did not have entrepreneurial experience, and 38% said their mentors did not provide concrete and actionable feedback.

In this study, it became evident that Indonesian EDPs struggle with two main issues: limited availability of mentors and limited range of expertise (see Appendixes for the complete lists of mentors).

Recommendations for Incubators
- Expand roster of mentors to sufficiently cater to all tenants, including both technical and business development needs.
- Work with public and private sectors to develop a network of experts across Indonesia that could be tapped as mentors as needed.
- Ensure mentorship and training programs support offbeat ideas and include consumer behavior research and creation of demand for new products and services.
- Ensure mentorship and training programs are needs-based and consider the unique needs of targeted start-ups.

Access to Relevant Mentors

At PENS Sky Venture, tenants had access only to facilitators who were under contract to offer their services for about 4 hours each month. This proved insufficient for the incubator's 11 tenants, which meant the start-ups had difficulties scheduling meetings and often communicated with the facilitators only through e-mail exchanges. This led to delays, causing some tenants to stay longer in the program than expected before graduating.

Even DIIB's roster of 15 mentors had difficulty catering to the incubator's 33 tenants, as they were all working on a part-time basis. The insufficiency is even more apparent when the size of some of the tenant teams—ranging from 33 to 50 members each—is factored in.

Beyond the number of mentors available and their accessibility, the limited range of expertise represented likewise created constraints. Some EDPs did not have mentors with the technical expertise needed to guide the start-ups on developing their innovative products or services, while others did not have enough mentors focused on the business development aspects.

For instance, PENS Sky's roster of facilitators was dominated by technical experts, which meant the start-ups did not get enough training or advice on business matters such as legal issues, marketing, finance, and human resources. As a result, some tenants were able to develop and produce their innovative products but struggled to connect with their target markets.

Table 5 shows DIIB's incubation process.

Table 5: Incubation Process at Directorate of Business Innovation and Incubation

3–4 months	2 years	Advanced
Pre Incubation • Tenants • Recruitments • Program • Socialization • Selection process • Workshop and assistance • Announcement • UI Preneur Camp (boot camp)	Early Incubation • Workshop (tax, digital marketing) • Business plan (BMC financial forecast) • Business legality Development • Intellectual property • Certification and standardization • Business consultation • Business matching/pitching Final Stage • Product • Commercialization • Partnership • Market development	Post Incubation • Expansion and development • National and international business network • Production • Monitoring and evaluation

BMC = business model canvas, UI = University of Indonesia.
Source: ADB. 2019. TA 9678-INO: Evaluation of Entrepreneurship Development Program, Final Report. Unpublished.

DIIB, on the other hand, has 10 of its 15 mentors covering various aspects of the business process—including marketing, human resources, and customer relationship—which tenants found beneficial, as many of them lacked capabilities in business development and marketing.

However, DIIB lacked mentors in other key areas. It had only two mentors for digital applications and none for technology development and technology transfer. It also had only one mentor each in entrepreneurship, enterprise value creation, finance, and legal framework. Its tenants found limited support for market and consumer research as well as new market development.

A network of experts could be developed across Indonesia that could be tapped by EDPs as needed to address the limited availability of mentors. This can be complemented by professionally trained in-house mentors who can coordinate and source technical expertise and resources.

In IncuBie, tenants benefit from close mentoring from experienced technologists in fisheries, agribusiness, mechanical engineering, food technology, and livestock, among others. The incubator also has part-time mentors with industry experience in online marketing and different areas of agro-related technology.

When a new batch of start-ups joins IncuBie, a team of mentors and trainers engage each tenant to understand their needs and problems. Based on this needs assessment, tenants receive training in management, entrepreneurship, legal aspects and marketing, product processing, and so on.

Figure 5: Incubation Process at IncuBie

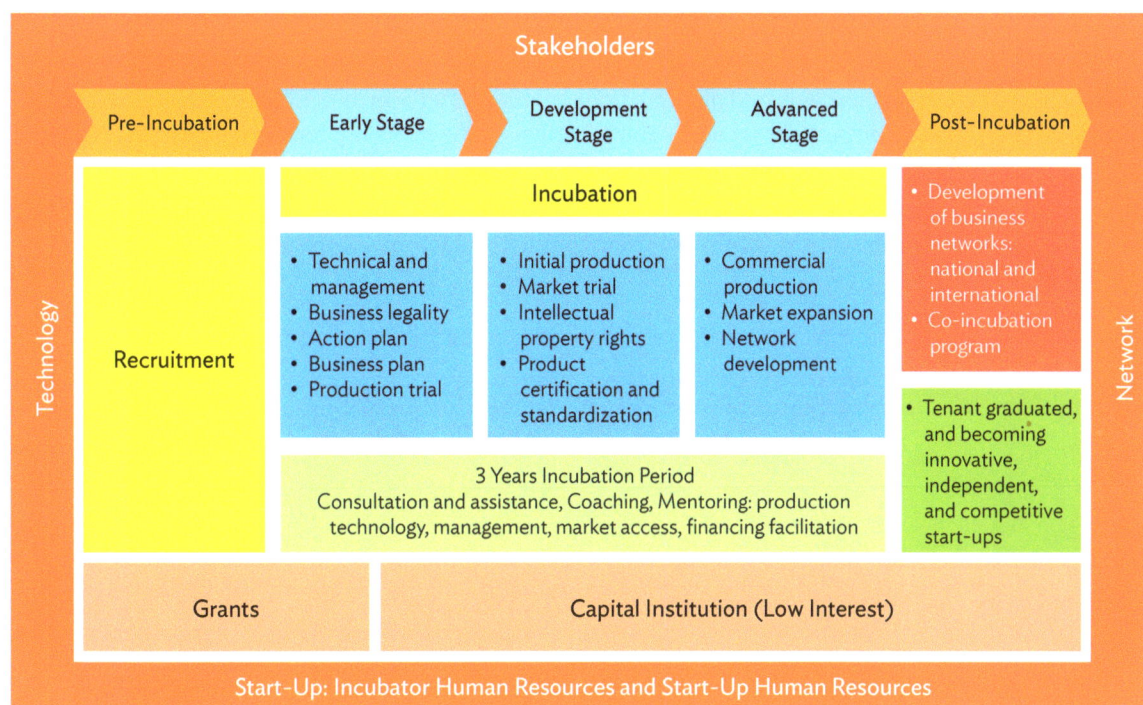

Stakeholders

Pre-Incubation	Early Stage	Development Stage	Advanced Stage	Post-Incubation

Technology

Incubation

Recruitment

- Technical and management
- Business legality
- Action plan
- Business plan
- Production trial

- Initial production
- Market trial
- Intellectual property rights
- Product certification and standardization

- Commercial production
- Market expansion
- Network development

- Development of business networks: national and international
- Co-incubation program

- Tenant graduated, and becoming innovative, independent, and competitive start-ups

Network

3 Years Incubation Period
Consultation and assistance, Coaching, Mentoring: production technology, management, market access, financing facilitation

Grants

Capital Institution (Low Interest)

Start-Up: Incubator Human Resources and Start-Up Human Resources

Source: ADB. 2019. TA 9678-INO: Evaluation of Entrepreneurship Development Program, Final Report. Unpublished.

The mentors and trainers also work with their assigned tenants to prepare action plans with key milestones, indicators, and a business plan. Whenever tenants are faced with new problems, they can also initiate brainstorming sessions with their mentors to find solutions.

Marketing Mentorship

However, as with PENS Sky and DIIB, IncuBie's mentorship program needs improvements in guiding tenants in marketing their innovations.

Although innovative products, by nature, often do not have a ready market, a common challenge seen among the EDPs studied is the limited mentorship provided on this specific start-up need—consumer behavior research and stimulating demand for new products and services through a behavior change campaign.

A few IncuBie tenants said they struggled to get favorable responses to their marketing campaigns, as they did not clearly understand their target groups and their aspirations toward the new products and services. Several tenants also said they struggled to justify their innovative business ideas, as their mentors wanted them to immediately identify who their consumers were.

Incubators must be able to help start-ups assess consumer perceptions of new ideas and concepts, as well as initiate behavior change communications and strategies to enter new markets with new products. Experts tapped as mentors should therefore also be experienced in providing a supportive environment for offbeat ideas and creating innovative enterprises.

Unique Needs

The kind of mentorship and expertise provided should consider not only the unique needs of innovative start-ups in general but also the specific needs of the EDP's tenants.

In AETP, high-profile and well-experienced mentors from Indonesia and Switzerland were recruited to prepare the tenants in their respective countries for internationalization (see Appendix 5 for the full list). The program was run concurrently in Indonesia and Switzerland with local trainers and coaches (Figure 6).

Figure 6: Asia Entrepreneurship Training Program for Acceleration Program

CURRICULUM	Pre-Training OPENING	PREPARATION	Full Day DAY 1	COACHING	Full Day DAY 2	COACHING	Full Day DAY 3	COACHING (summr braek)	Full Day DAY 4	COACHING	Full Day DAY 5	COACHING	Grand Final ROADSHOW/PITCHES
Morning (4-hour module) 8 a.m.–12 noon	15 MARCH ZURICH / JAKARTA		Session 1.0 Introduction and fund raising for your international venture (team entry pitches-1)		Session 3.0 Analysis of your target Asian market		Session 5.0 Building your international business model		Session 7.0 Market entry and road map		Session 9.0 Pitching		Start-up exchange: Selected CH start-ups will travel to Asia and vice versa
Coffee and lunch provided	Joint Opening Ceremony in Zurich in Zurich (a.m.) and Jakarta (p.m.) - linked through teleconference												
Afternoon (4-hour module) 2 p.m.–6 p.m.			Session 2.0 Internationalization strategies and cultural considerations (team entry pitches-2)		Session 4.0 Value proposition for your new markt		Session 6.0 Develop your team and overseas partnership		Session 8.0 Raising finance and pitching for international growth		Session 10.0 Building your network		
Coffee and lunch provided			Evening event				Final decision (internal)						

Notes:
1. The program consists of 5 full-day training days with two 4-hour modules a.m./p.m. and weekly in between.
2. Same schedule runs concurrently in Indonesia and Switzerland, delivered by local trainers or coaches.
3. Session and pitches will be video recorded for feedback.
4. Between training days, the teams will work independently, supported by a coach.

Source: ADB. 2019. TA 9678-INO: Evaluation of Entrepreneurship Development Program, Final Report. Unpublished.

During 9 months, the tenants received 5 training days, covering topics such as fundraising, internationalization strategies and cultural considerations, building an international business model, overseas partnerships, market entry, and pitching for international growth. Between the training days, the teams worked independently and were supported by a coach as they worked toward internationalization.

However, there was no exchange of mentors to train and coach tenants from the other country. Consequently, the tenants found the mentorship and training provided to be too theoretical, with no real-life experience in the markets and production realities of the two countries.

After the training was completed, the tenants made their pitches and the selected winners advanced to the next step for internationalization—going to Switzerland or Indonesia to pitch to investors. The Swiss tenants quickly realized, though, that the start-up scene in Indonesia was very different from their own. In Switzerland, infrastructure, institutions, and other support systems were available to start-ups even at the development stage. But though they had everything they needed, Swiss start-ups were not too interested in taking risks. On the other hand, the more youthful Indonesian entrepreneurs showed greater passion and risk appetite than their Swiss counterparts.

Ideally, the Swiss start-ups seeking to expand to Indonesia should have Indonesian mentors and trainers, and vice versa. The key focus of mentorship should be the realignment of business registration, acquiring licenses and permits, and finding local partners.

Access to Business Services and Facilities

Aside from gaining access to mentors, start-ups also need access to business services, production facilities, technology, and other resources that can help them develop their products and services without incurring substantial costs.

On this aspect, IncuBie's facilities and infrastructure stand out. Its tenants can conduct all their key business operations using the center's high-quality equipment and technology at low costs. Aside from providing the usual meeting and training rooms with internet connectivity, IncuBie has space to host 15 tenants as well as food production and packaging equipment and machineries such as an evaporator and condenser. But with the growing demand of IncuBie's new start-ups, the center needs to add space and modernize its facilities (see Appendixes for the complete lists of facilities).

Recommendations for Incubators
- Ensure sufficient office space and infrastructure to support the development of products and services.
- Provide business services such as business registration, permits, licenses, etc.

Provision of the right mentor, facilities, and timely support helped Ecodoe—a start-up that focuses on handicrafts—turn into a viable business (Box 2).

Aside from providing facilities, IncuBie can also help tenants prepare their business plans and provide consultation for technical production and business management.

Its tenants say they have benefitted immensely from the incubator's office and storage spaces, communications facilities, designing and packaging tools, and technology and production infrastructure. All these reduced the amount of investments they needed to make in their own businesses.

PENS Sky Venture also offered tenants working spaces and basic production facilities, but these were more limited than what IncuBie has. While it has meeting spaces, internet connection, and communications equipment, they were not enough to cater to all its tenants. The start-ups also must share PENS Sky's laboratory and testing equipment, production facilities, and design studio with other PENS students, creating long waits. Often, tenants found the equipment they needed either unavailable or not working.

Also, business development services were not delivered satisfactorily due to the absence of a technical team in start-up creation and management.

Despite its good support for research ideas, DIIB offers very limited technology and infrastructure for creating new products. Therefore, tenants have to look for this outside DIIB, which can be costly and time-consuming.

At AETP, product development was another key support that worked in favor of the tenants as they had access to facilities for technical research, product testing, and design. Tenants also immensely benefitted from infrastructure facilities such as office, communication, designing, packaging, technology, and production including a storage facility.

Box 2: Ecodoe: Mentorship for a Crucial Pivot

Shortly after launching Ecodoe in 2014 as a business producing souvenirs made of natural materials, it seemed as though everything was going well for Larasati Widyaputri and her cofounder.

"The idea came simply when I traveled to Yogyakarta and dropped by a souvenir sellers center at Kasongan. I met a crafter who had just lost her husband after the Yogyakarta earthquake. She was struggling to have a stable livelihood," she said.

The following year, Ecodoe was one of four teams to win a S$10,000 grant from the 2015 Young Social Entrepreneur organized by the Singapore International Foundation. The process gave the pair international exposure as well as access to coaching from McKinsey & Company. They even went on a social entrepreneurship study visit to Mumbai, India.

But by 2017, with her cofounder taking the lead, the company found itself in trouble. "We seemed to be over hiring, over borrowing, and overstocked, because we hired our own production division despite the fact that we still had not found our product–market fit," she said.

"Soon the cash burned out, and he did not want be responsible for the company anymore. I needed to lay off 70% of my team, shut down the production department, shut down all the offline shops, and move to a cheaper flat as our new office."

Larasati realized she had to change their business model. Remembering their study visit to Mumbai, where they saw locals producing bags that were sold all over the world through Amazon, she decided to turn Ecodoe into an e-commerce platform for gifts and souvenirs.

But she knew little about the world of e-commerce and decided to look for mentorship and apply for a grant from the Ministry of Research, Technology and Higher Education.

"When I was applying, I received guidance and was reviewed by IncuBie, since I'm an alumnus [of the Bogor Agricultural University]," she said, adding that the reviewers at the time already advised that they pivot from a business-to-consumer model to a business-to-business model.

However, IncuBie was fully occupied at the time and so Ecodoe was assigned to another business incubator, UBpreneur, the Bakrie family's incubator in Jakarta.

"The very first time I met with the mentor from UBpreneur, he immediately gave me access to the idle office space behind his house in Mampang, Jakarta. He also connected me with a coach in digital marketing, where we got intensive weekly training in internet marketing," she said.

With proper mentoring and guidance, Ecodoe's pivot worked. Within a year, it saw its sales grow by more than 800%.

"Last year, we even received inquiries for 50 million pieces of souvenirs," she said. "We are eager to scale up our impact further."

Source: ADB. 2019. TA 9678-INO: Evaluation of Entrepreneurship Development Program, Final Report. Unpublished.

Access to Funding

Helping tenants gain increased access to investment capital is another service provided by incubators that studies have found to be statistically significantly related to the performance of start-ups.

According to ANGIN, 50% of start-ups are looking for investment when they join EDPs, with 32% of them receiving follow-on funding within 2 years of program participation. Of those who received the follow-on funding, about half credited it to the EDPs.

Our study also found that while most EDPs provide initial funding, start-ups need guidance on how to efficiently use these grants and training on how to prepare investment proposals to secure additional financing in the future.

At DIIB, all accepted tenants receive seed financial grants from UI to carry on their start-up activities. In addition, MOECRT also considers selected tenants for grants of a minimum of $20,000 based on their proposals. Tenants also receive assistance in finding other investors and in networking within the national and global markets.

However, not all DIIB tenants can use these funds efficiently and for expenses relevant to their start-ups since there is little guidance on how to use them.

At IncuBie, tenants receive guidance in preparing financial proposals to be submitted to MOECRT, with about half receiving about $21,500 in funding each. Those not chosen can get seed funding from the university but often just to cover 10% of their proposed amount. Therefore, they would have to seek the balance from other sources, for which they need guidance in preparing winning investment proposals.

However, IncuBie does not have a strong network of angel investors, venture capitalists, financial collaborators, and partners, limiting the options for where tenants can obtain much-needed financing.

At PENS Sky Venture, tenants are also offered financial assistance during their incubation period and can apply for the same $20,000 grant from MOECRT. PENS also provides grants but only to its students if they are selected for incubation. MOECRT also shares 25% of the total grant provided to each tenant to cover the cost of incubation activities and other overhead expenses.

Recommendations for Incubators
- Provide guidance on how to prepare winning investment proposals.
- Provide guidance on how to use funding grants efficiently.

Graduation and Post-Incubation

If start-ups are subjected to stringent criteria before being accepted to EDPs, they should meet clear exit criteria before graduation. According to the US study, incubation programs with lax or no exit policies typically have less-than-optimal performance.

The qualifications for when tenants can graduate should be clearly defined, and assessment systems should be established to ensure stability, growth, and sustainability after they leave. For example, assessing the tenant's readiness to implement growth plans should be a key requirement for graduation.

Recommendations for Incubators
- Establish clear exit criteria for graduation, including readiness to implement growth plans.
- Provide post-incubation services such as access to specialized facilities as needed, consulting services, chief executive officer roundtables, and networking functions.

At IncuBie, tenants are regularly assessed based on standard operating procedures and key performance indicators. If they meet their key performance indicators before the 3-year incubation period is completed, they are allowed to graduate and enter the post-incubation process for establishing linkages with the foreign market.

However, IncuBie graduates have indicated that they realized they lacked the capacity to cope with the growth of their sales, operations, and team.

At DIIB, after completing a 1-year incubation period, tenants are supposed to graduate and exit. However, they can apply for an extension if needed. If granted, they can stay for a maximum period of 1 year, although with limited assistance. Unfortunately, this means they will not get any additional funding from the university, and they may not get an office space and a mentor.

After they graduate, the start-ups can again apply for post-incubation, which involves expansion, national and international business networking, production support, and further monitoring and evaluation.

Box 3: eGURU ALMaS: Starting with Zero Knowledge

When Ali Ishaq decided to become an entrepreneur in 2016, he did not know much about running a business but knew a lot about what teachers need.

Having worked as a high school teacher in a private high school in Probolinggo, East Java for 5 years until 2012, he was aware that the job involved many complex and time-consuming administrative tasks. At the time, he started developing an application based on Microsoft Excel to help teachers manage these tasks, so that they can free up time to focus more on the actual job of teaching.

So when he decided to go into business in 2016, he dusted off the application he was working on and set out to improve it.

"After I perfected one, a high school in Gresik became the first buyer of my application. After that, more and more schools became interested in the application, which was named eGURU ALMaS," he said.

The eGURU ALMaS application aids teachers by automating the monitoring and assessment of student learning outcomes using various parameters in line with Indonesian education standards. Through the application, teachers can conduct a complex and integrated assessment of their students' competencies in terms of knowledge, skills, and attitudes.

In 2019, he received a grant from the Ministry of Research, Technology and Higher Education to develop eGURU ALMaS into a viable business, and he joined PENS Sky Venture as a tenant.

"From this incubation, I gained a lot of knowledge about business management and business development," he said.

In particular, he learned about branding and marketing and the basics of management—topics he did not learn as a nursing student.

"All ecosystems and communities in PENS Sky Venture support each other and help each other to progress together."

Source: ADB. 2019. TA 9678-INO: Evaluation of Entrepreneurship Development Program, Final Report. Unpublished.

EDPs can also continue to provide services to graduates, such as access to specialized facilities as needed, consulting services, chief executive officer roundtables, and networking functions.

Incubators should provide mentorship, knowledge, and guidance on various aspects of business, including marketing, financial management, and product development. Box 3 reveals how a tenant is able to turn an idea into a real business.

Institutional Improvements

Documentation and Evaluation

International studies show that a business incubator's success is strongly tied to the outcomes of its clients and graduates. The strong reputations of DIIB and IncuBie, for example, stem largely from the success of its graduates. In fact, a coffee table book documenting DIIB's tenants and their products is credited for inspiring other start-ups to apply for incubation as well.

Recommendations for Incubators
- Keep track of graduates and collect data on performance.
- Analyze collected data regularly to use as basis for evaluating incubation services and programs.

At the same time, an evaluation of the performance of their graduates can help improve the programs and processes of incubators. According to the Thai study, their business incubators assessed their performance on factors such as the creation and growth of new businesses, their impact on the economy, their tenants' return on investment, and their graduates' survival rate (footnote 11). Demonstrating a positive return on incubators' investment in start-ups can consequently strengthen public funding support.

Therefore, once tenants graduate, incubation centers must regularly keep track of them and note their progress to validate their services, showcase successes, and learn from failures.

According to the US study, two-thirds of high-achieving incubators collect client outcome data more often and for longer periods than their peers (footnote 9). The data include revenues and employment, survival rates, and the outcome of specific programs and activities. More than half collect this information for 2 or more years, while over 30% collect it for 5 or more years.

These data can be collected at least annually from the graduates and then analyzed every 3–5 years to serve as the basis for evaluating the incubator's programs and processes. Ideally, according to the US study, this evaluation should be linked to the incubator's public funding.

Developing a Strong Network

Recommendation for Incubators
- Develop and leverage strong network within academic and business communities, as well as with government agencies and state-owned enterprises to create a strong ecosystem. Accomplishing this will require the support and participation of their parent institutions and the government through the Ministry of Education and Culture and Ministry of Research, Technology and Higher Education.

Effective EDPs do not just provide free office space and training to start-ups, they also provide business matching and networking support, assist in obtaining grants or financing from financial institutions or investors, and help start-ups access public agencies and gain support from the wider academic and business community, according to the Thai study (footnote 11).

But EDPs can only do these if they have strong networks within the academic and business communities, as well as with government agencies. The US study defined incubation programs as offering business support and services both in the incubator and through its network of contacts.

In this regard, DIIB stands out by having a good network in the start-up community, venture capitalists, state-owned companies, and other support groups in both the private and public sectors. This allows it to easily reach out for support as well as for sourcing public funds.

UI's large academic community means a significant number of its members can provide services at the different stages of incubation. Its alumni and lecturers support DIIB tenants through networking, business proposals, mentorship, and training as key speakers.

DIIB's partnership with some start-up studios—Badr Start-up Studio, Bukalapak Start-ups, Blibli.com—is also advantageous, as these enterprises can offer mentorship and training (Table 6). Relationships with MOECRT, state-owned banks like Bank Mandiri and BNI, as well as BEEHIVE (Building Entrepreneurial Ecosystems to Enhance Higher Education Value-Added for Better Graduate Employability) have been very helpful terms of accessing funding and equipment for tenants.

Table 6: Stakeholders and Partners of Directorate of Business Innovation and Incubation

Partners and Collaborators	Services and Support
UI researchers, lecturers, inventors	Knowledge, training, and mentorship
MOECRT	Knowledge, training, and mentorship
Bank Mandiri	Sponsors competition for start-ups
Bank Negara Indonesia	Networking and funding for coworking space
ILUNI UI (UI Alumni)	Networking and key speakers
Badr Start-up Studio	Mentorship
AIBI (Incubator Association)	Networking and information
Business (practitioners)	Key speakers
Bukalapak	Key speakers
Blibli.com	Start-up in marketplace
Asian Business Incubator Network	Networking, funding for events, knowledge
BEEHIVE (Building Entrepreneurship)	Computers and other equipment
Other incubators	Joint programs

MOECRT = Ministry of Education, Culture, Research, and Technology.
Source: ADB. 2019. TA 9678-INO: Evaluation of Entrepreneurship Development Program, Final Report. Unpublished.

This was an advantage enjoyed by ATM Sehat, a start-up established by Sigit Nuzul while he was a UI student incubated at DIIB (Box 1). Through the UI academic network, he found a partner, an adviser, and a chief executive officer. He found experts to help improve his device prototype, as well as access to various state-owned and private companies that eventually became partners.

The start-up is now working with state-owned company PT Mitra Rajawali Banjaran to produce the ATM Sehat devices that offer remote medical services in poor and disadvantaged communities, with PT Rajawali Nusindo for selling the devices through its nationwide network of branches, and with PT Kimia Farma for health consultations by doctors in their clinics.

Even after tenants graduate, access to DIIB's vast network can still serve as an important resource for start-ups. EDPs can leverage this network to offer attractive post-incubation services like chief executive officer roundtables and networking functions.

A strong network can also compensate for an incubator's shortcomings. In the case of PENS Sky Venture, for instance, the industry connections of its parent institution, PENS, worked as a strong support to its tenants, providing the start-ups with technology and marketing assistance. The incubator also helped its tenants raise capital funds through the PENS network.

Some IncuBie tenants have also lauded IPB's large network and reputation in the agriculture sector, which helped them get easy access to relevant stakeholders. This includes access to the international market and export support, including international business-to-business contracts.

However, tenants have noted that IncuBie needs to further develop its network of venture capitalists, angel investors, and financial collaborators not only within Indonesia but also globally to offer more options for funding.

Appendix 1

Perception of Tenants		DIIB	IncuBie	PENS Sky
Technological Idea Development Support and Process		**70.6**	**78.0**	**65.0**
1	Culture for creating offbeat ideas	76.7	85.0	58.5
2	Opportunities for creating innovative ideas or finding creative solutions to problems	70.0	85.0	67.1
3	Support for creating/designing new products and services	70.0	75.0	69.3
4	Idea research for concept discovering and validation of the concept	80.0	72.5	58.7
5	Development of technology and infrastructure for creating a new product in a lab	50.0	75.0	61.5
6	Support of a multidisciplinary mentorship team	76.7	77.5	74.7
Market Development		**61.3**	**78.0**	**65.6**
7	Facilities for product testing and creating effective operations for production systems	53.3	75.0	60.0
8	Mentorship for reaching out and market working out: costing, pricing, packaging, and delivery to ultimate consumers	63.3	82.5	68.0
9	Opportunities for market study on consumer behavior	60.0	75.0	54.7
10	Support for preparing marketing communications campaign for accepting new products	66.7	77.5	70.7
11	Mentorship and networking usefulness in market channels establishment	63.3	80.0	74.7
Business Development Services		**78.9**	**82.5**	**64.1**
12	Coaching services, needs-based	73.3	80.0	66.7
13	Training on entrepreneurial capacity building	83.3	82.5	61.3
14	Business extension services (accounting, legal, secretarial support, etc.)	80.0	85.0	64.3
Capacity Development for Sustainability and Growth		**69.8**	**76.0**	**59.2**
15	Help in finding cofounder/corporate founder/partner or investors	66.7	75.0	54.7
16	Adequate training and mentorship for building the management team	70.0	75.0	65.3
17	Mentorship helpfulness in preparing a milestone-based plan	60.0	72.5	66.7
18	Support commitment or mobilization of resources as per the milestone	66.7	72.5	60.0

continued on next page

Table A1.1 continued

	Perception of Tenants	DIIB	IncuBie	PENS Sky
19	Provide market research support adequately	63.3	77.5	52.0
20	Providing product market/consumer creation for new product	56.7	65.0	57.1
21	Guidance in scaling-up strategy	63.3	82.5	60.0
22	Facilitation for accessing public business development funds	83.3	80.0	66.7
23	Network of private investors (business angels, venture capitalists)	76.7	70.0	43.1
24	Guidance for preparation of their projects to start-up venture financing	73.3	67.5	52.0
25	Training and advisory services on building strategic business partnerships	76.7	82.5	60.0
26	Organization of regular (e.g., weekly or biweekly) networking meetings for tenants and investors/prospective business partners	66.7	77.5	65.3
27	Training in organizational systems for sustaining business	73.3	85.0	62.7
28	Training in leadership for leading an organizational entity	80.0	82.5	62.7
	Total (%)	**70.1**	**78.6**	**63.4**

Source: ADB. 2020. Evaluation of Entrepreneurship Development Program in Indonesia. Final Report. TA 9678-INO: Advanced Knowledge and Skills for Sustainable Growth. Unpublished.

Appendix 2

IncuBie Tenants and Services

Table A2.1: Profiles of Selected IncuBie Tenants

Name and Company	Date of Joining	Date of Launch	Business Activities	Turnover and % of Profit Turnover	Employees	Innovation
Iqbal, Muhammad Hafid – PT BIKI	2019	2018	Functional food and health	$14,000/year, 25%	15	Healthy food made from Chitosan
Andika, Gema Sukmawati – PT Interstisi	2018	2017	Manufacturing	$21,500/year, 20%	3 (many outsourced)	Green composite helmet, made from empty bunch palm fruit: very strong, very light, and eco-friendly
Lina Shabrina, Osephire, Masker from spirulina	2019	2019	Creative industry (cosmetics)	$350/month, 25%–30%	2	Cosmetics made from spirulina with a better smell
Tedi, Liza – CV Wain	2019	2018	Healthy Food	$6,000/month, 20%–25%	11 and 40 farmers	Breast milk production booster made from Torbangun leaves
Indra Thamrin – Yourtea	2013	2008	Food	$2,500/month, 15%	40	Various types of tea, best quality with lowest price, franchising
Sri Hidayat – CV Madu Apiari	2014	2011	Food	$470,000/year, 20%	25	Natural honey with various flavors, honey derivative products: soap, shampoo, candy, propolis
Larasati Widyaputri –Ecodoe	2017	2016	Handicraft information and communication technology (ICT)-based e-commerce	$250,000/year, 30%–40%	11, with 400 local creators	E-commerce platform for handicrafts

Source: ADB. 2020. Evaluation of Entrepreneurship Development Program in Indonesia. Final Report. TA 9678-INO: Advanced Knowledge and Skills for Sustainable Growth. Unpublished.

Table A2.2: Mentors and Trainers

Names of Mentors	Nature of Association of Incubation	Key Area of Expertise/ Experience	Key Achievements/Impact on Start-Ups
Davit	RWP Group	Online marketing	Has helped hundreds of mentees (start-ups, companies) in increasing product sales using an e-commerce system (digital marketing)
Fikri Azali	IncuBie	Mechanical engineering and biosystems	Has helped mentees in developing products and packaging
Annisa Nurul (Nisa)	IncuBie	Marketing and business management	Has helped mentees increase product sales by offline and online marketing, and business management
Dadang Tresna	IncuBie	Food technology	Has helped mentees in developing their products, formulation, and good manufacturing practice (GMP)
Muhamad Alfian	IncuBie	Product certification and business legal	Has helped hundreds of mentees in product certification and business legality

Source: ADB. 2020. Evaluation of Entrepreneurship Development Program in Indonesia. Final Report. TA 9678-INO: Advanced Knowledge and Skills for Sustainable Growth. Unpublished.

Table A2.3: Infrastructure and Facilities

S.N.	Facilities, Technical Equipment, Offices Spaces	Number
1	Land at STP IPB Taman Kencana	1
2	Management office STP IPB Taman Kencana	1
3	Technical Facilities	
	3.1. Management office	3
	3.2. Meeting room	1
	3.3. In-wall tenant room	6
	3.4. Design center	1
	3.5. Breakout room (Relaks)	1
4	Operations/Productions	
	4.1. Basement: animal lab	1
	a. Operational room	20
	b. Supporting room	10
	4.2. 1st floor: management Science Techno Park	1
	a. STP management office	1
	b. Technology Transfer office	1
	c. Training room	4
	4.3. 2nd floor 2: Biofarmaka	1
	a. Operational room	22
	b. Supporting room	10

continued on next page

Table A2.3 continued

S.N.	Facilities, Technical Equipment, Offices Spaces	Number
	4.4. 3rd floor: office and labs	1
	a. Operational room	9
	b. Supporting room	9
	4.5. 4th floor: office and labs	1
	a. Operational room	9
	b. Supporting room	6
5	Pilot plant	1
6	Guesthouse	2
7	Restaurant	1
8	Animal clinic	1
9	Parking lot	3
10	Offices spaces (1)	1
	10.1. Management room	4
	10.2. In-wall room	1
	10.3. Multifunction room	
11	Coworking space TechnosNet	1
12	Office spaces (2)	
	12.1. Management room	1
	12.2. In-wall room	12
	12.3. Meeting room	1
13	Machineries	
	13.1. Extractor SUS 304: Cap.	
	13.2. Evaporator SUS 304: Cap.	
	13.3. Condenser SUS 304: Cap.	
	13.4. Boiler SUS 304: Cap. 13.5	
	13.5. Cooling Tower SUS 304	
14	Food production facilities and packaging	
	14.1. Vacuum frying	
	14.2. Vacuum packing	
	14.3. Freeze drying	
	14.4. Coding batch code and expired date	
	14.5. Plastic bottle capping	
	14.6. Metal bottle capping	
15	Teaching farm laboratory: production of horticulture, education, and marketing	
16	Closed house system Cultivation of chicken Working together with PT. Charoen Pokphand Indonesia, Tbk	

Source: ADB. 2020. Evaluation of Entrepreneurship Development Program in Indonesia. Final Report. TA 9678-INO: Advanced Knowledge and Skills for Sustainable Growth. Unpublished.

Appendix 3

PENS Sky Venture Tenants and Services

Table A3.1: Profiles of Selected PENS Sky Venture Tenants

Name and Designation	Date of Joining	Date of Launch	Business Activities	Turnover and Return %
Audrey Maximillian Herli, cofounder of Riliv	2018	2015	Connecting people with personal problems to a professional psychologist, provide online guided meditation content	Undisclosed for public or media
Florencia, founder	Mar 2019	Feb 2017	Parenting platform—psychologists and experts to support millennial parents on their parenting journey. The product is Kelas Ortu, a series of online parenting classes.	$7,000; No profits yet, but also no deficits
ALI ISHAQ, Founder eGURU ALMaS	Apr 2019	Jan 2016	B2C with schools in Indonesia	$7,000; 70% profit
Riza Yulian	Mar 2018	Dec 2017	Device production, partnership, selling (description on the writing)	2018: $1,300; 50% profit 2019: $1,400; 60% profit
Cahyo Sugianto, CEO, PT Nasta Mekatronika Indonesia	Mar 2019	Apr 2016	Production, selling, maintenance, and Retrovit Automatic Guided, Vehicle Robot	$20,0000; 32% profit
Dhadhang SBW, CEO, Surovotic	Feb 2019	2017	SUROVOTIC is a portable underwater robot, the main business in renting remotely operated vehicle (ROV) to companies or for personal use	–
M Miftahul Huda, CEO, PT Cipta Media Edutama	Apr 2019	Jul 2016	Work together with schools using partnerships in the form of software as a service. Promote the business using online and offline media, and hold seminars in schools.	$10,000 40% profit
Bidya Nur Habib, CAHLURAH	2018		Researching, analyzing, evaluating, promoting, branding, eggshell breaking, and egg yolk separator	
Rizky Kurniawan, CEO Tempe Niza	Apr 2019	Dec 2018	Hygienic tempe processing machines (soybean breaking machines, yeast mixing machines, and measuring machines)	$1,075; 30% profit
Surya Adi Wijaya, Founder and CEO Tepat Guna Tech	Apr 2016	May 2015	3D printer manufacture (Acrobat), 3D printing services, 3D design services, 3D design and printing training	$17,000; 69%–72% profit over turnover

Source: ADB. 2020. Evaluation of Entrepreneurship Development Program in Indonesia. Final Report. TA 9678-INO: Advanced Knowledge and Skills for Sustainable Growth. Unpublished.

Table A3.2: Facilitators

Facilitators	Nature of Association for Incubation	Key Areas of Expertise/ Experience	Key Achievements/Impact on Start-Ups
Yoki	Part-time	Digital software (Ui/Ux)	Managing tenant's mindset to be prepared or survive for a longer time in the future
Awan	Part-time	Instrumentation	Business planning
Wira Syahputra	Part-time	Digital software (marketing)	Giving examples of other start-ups to the tenants to inspire them
Zainal	Part-time	Digital software	Managing the mortgage from the government

Source: ADB. 2020. Evaluation of Entrepreneurship Development Program in Indonesia. Final Report. TA 9678-INO: Advanced Knowledge and Skills for Sustainable Growth. Unpublished.

Table A3.3: Facilities

Facilities	Description	Challenges
In-wall incubation	Maximum 16	Limited space and very crowded
Out-wall incubation	Offered meeting halls for use, also used by PENS Sky Venture as the corporate address	
Coworking space	Located near the main tenants' office	Multipurpose use of facilities
Office equipment (common facilities)	Tenants are provided office equipment like computer, printer, chair, whiteboard, projectors, stationery, and Internet.	These equipment are limited and cannot be provided to everyone adequately. The Internet has limited bandwidth.
Laboratory, prototyping, or testing equipment	Tenants can use all tools that PENS has.	On sharing equipment with all of the students from PENS. A lot of the equipment do not work well.
Production facilities or equipment Design studio	Tenants can use all tools that PENS has (Parent).	Sharing equipment with all of PENS students, making tenants wait for their turn
Technology transfer	With the support of PENS alumnus	Tenants sometimes have very different fields from the alumni
Pilot plant	Available from pre-incubation to post-incubation	No one to supervise
Research Center	Tenants can use rooms of PENS	Sharing basis
Meeting rooms and training hall	One meeting room and one training hall	Limited to one meeting and training hall, tenants have to wait for their turn

Source: ADB. 2020. Evaluation of Entrepreneurship Development Program in Indonesia. Final Report. TA 9678-INO: Advanced Knowledge and Skills for Sustainable Growth. Unpublished.

Appendix 4

Directorate of Business Innovation and Incubation Tenants and Services

Table A4.1: Awards Won by Directorate of Business Innovation and Incubation Tenants

No.	Name	Firms	Award
2015			
1	Eng. Muhamad Sahlan, S.Si, M. Eng.	CV. Nano Biotek Indonesia	The Asian Bowl Start-Up Awards 2015 finalist in the university start-up category
2016			
2	Anju Hasiholan Daniel Pasaribu	PT. Belimbing Island Indonesia	Best Tenants in Health and Medicine in I3E 2016
3	Adi Lingson and Sanlaruska Fathernas	PT. Juragan Kapal Indonesia (Kapal Pelat Datar)	Industry Technology Pioneer Award (Rintisan Teknologi Industri, RINTEK) Ministry of Industry 2016
2017			
4	Agung Hartansyah	PT Rekayasa Energi Global	National Finalist of Independent Young Entrepreneurs 2016
5	Anju Hasiholan Daniel Pasaribu	PT. Belimbing Island Indonesia	UKM Wow 2017 (SMEs Wow 2017) from the Ministry of Cooperatives and SME Republic of Indonesia at the 2017 SME Festival
			The Most Attractive Booth of the Day from the Indonesian Ministry of Cooperatives and SMEs at the 2017 SME Festival
			The Best Sales of The Day from Indonesian Ministry of Cooperatives and SMEs at the 2017 SME Festival
6	Restu Alan Suyuti	Pervious Pavement	Participant in the National Habitat Day event of the Directorate General of Human Settlements of the Ministry of PUPR RI
7	Ferry Alif Purnama Sugandhi	PT Infishta Digital Indonesia	Best Paper in the 16th Sharia Economics Days FEB UI
8	Imam Askolani	PT Weston Integrasi Energi	Plug and Play Finalist Pitching Presentation

continued on next page

Table A4.1 continued

No.	Name	Firms	Award
9	Ahmad Zaki Anshori	PT Tele Sehat Indonesia	Workshop on Technology Commercialization in London, UK with the title "Leadership in Innovation Fellowship" program
10	Aji Teguh Prihatno	PT Jaya Otomasi Solusindo	Workshop on Technology Commercialization in London, UK with the title "Leadership in Innovation Fellowship" program
11	Fahmy Fil Ardhy Nurwantara	PT Tasawa Herbal Nusantara	Workshop on Technology Commercialization in London, UK with the title "Leadership in Innovation Fellowship" program
12	Gohan Parningotan	Sikomo	The 1st best Indosat Hackathon 2017
2018			
13	Fahmy Fil Ardhi Nurwantara	PT Tasawa Herbal Nusantara	LIF London, Royal Academy of Engineering
14	Ferry Alif Purnama Sugandhi	PT Infishta Digital Indonesia	Finalist WMM Mandiri in Fintech category
15	Ahmad Zaki Anshori	PT Tele Sehat Indonesia	Korea's ICT Global Start-up Program 2018
16	Khaira Al Hafi	PT Meetchange Kolaborasi Indonesia	Best National Digital Solution for International World Summits Awards in the Category
17	Amsa Mustaqim	PT POCI Otomasi Cerdas Indonesia	3rd Place in the NYALA Smart Energy Hackathon 2018
2019			
18	Ferry Alif Purnama Sugandhi	PT Infishta Digital Indonesia	First Place in the royal academy of engineering's leaders in innovation fellowships (final pitch session) 2019
19	Regita Sari Cahya	PT Tele Sehat Indonesia	Silver Medal - I3F 2019, Malang
20	Yolla Miranda	PT Sainsgo Karya Indonesia	Gold Medal - I3F 2019, Malang
21	M. Arifin Julian	Creafta B-ionik	2nd Place at the 2019 International Science and Invention Fair
22	Christian Hutabarat	Dukungcalonmu.com	1st Best Pitch, BEEHIVE International Pitch Event, Manila
23	Mochammad Auditya Brilliant	FK Tanpa Batas	3rd Best Pitch, BEEHIVE International Pitch Event, Manila
24	Eghar Anugrapaksi	KLEMM	Best Banner Design, BEEHIVE International Pitch Event, Manila
25	M. Arifin Julian	Creafta B-ionik	Gold Medal, World Convention and Exhibition 2019, Malaysia
26	Ahmad Zaki Anshori	PT Tele Sehat Indonesia	Gold Medal - ASEAN ICT Award 2019 R&D Category

Source: ADB. 2020. Evaluation of Entrepreneurship Development Program in Indonesia. Final Report. TA 9678-INO: Advanced Knowledge and Skills for Sustainable Growth. Unpublished.

Table A4.2: Mentors

No.	Name	Expertise
	Digital Application	
1	Ardi Alhaidar	Software development/programming
2	Wahyu Rismawan	Software engineering, web technology, mobile development
	Entrepreneurship and Management	
3	Arry Rahmawan	Self-development, technology entrepreneurship, and management
4	Yuszak M. Yahya	Change management, financial modeling, enterprise value creation, and troubleshooting
	Finance	
5	Abidah Syauqina	Finance
	Business Development, Marketing, and Customer Relations	
6	Andreas Senjaya	Pitching, growth hacking, profit generating, marketing strategy, leadership
7	Topan Bayu Kusuma	Business development, application development
8	Big Zaman	Project management, computer science, leadership
9	Fahry Yanuar Rahman	Brand development
10	Rahardian Wahyu Pradana	Human resource, digital marketing, user experience, product campaign
11	Iqbal Hariadi	Marketing strategy, content creating
12	Susanto No More	Marketing strategy
13	Asril Fitri Syamas	Business development and risk monitoring
14	Siska Indah Pratiwi	Customer relations, community culture, growth hacking, marketing strategy
	Legal Business Entity	
15	Grace Monika Ramli	Legal business entity

Source: ADB. 2020. Evaluation of Entrepreneurship Development Program in Indonesia. Final Report. TA 9678-INO: Advanced Knowledge and Skills for Sustainable Growth. Unpublished.

Table A4.3: Facilities

Facilities	Uses of the Facilities
Cubicles	24 for 24 tenants
In-wall incubation	Programmed throughout
Coworking space	Available in an open space next to the cubicles
Two meeting rooms	Capacity 15 and 20 persons LCD projector and whiteboard
Training hall	150 persons
Office equipment	Refrigerator and water dispenser Printers
Common facilities (available for up to 28 persons)	Internet, Wi-Fi (up to 100 Mbps) Labs are shared with other departments depending on the availability of prototyping, testing faculty, or departments of UI
Equipment	Production facilities 3D printers Offset printer

Source: ADB. 2020. Evaluation of Entrepreneurship Development Program in Indonesia. Final Report. TA 9678-INO: Advanced Knowledge and Skills for Sustainable Growth. Unpublished.

Appendix 5

Asia Entrepreneurship Training Program Tenants and Services

Table A5.1: Swiss Tenants

Company/Team Leaders	Proposal	Comments
Aventura.aero AG Daniel Y. Spring	Invented and developed the affordable and powerful heavy-duty gyrocopter, aventura.aero.	AG aims for the huge market in developing nations by providing a cost-efficient alternative to helicopters. Unique in its kind, the heavy-duty gyrocopter is suitable for surveillance, disaster relief, and urgent transport with a market potential of beyond 2,500 units per year.
Pracman AG Simon Bless, Purushartha Saini	Medical doctors and alternative physicians need an efficient admin software with a holistic history view of patient data.	Worldwide, most inputs happen on paper, but the output needs to be digital. Our calendar-centric practice management application offers ultrafast, unmatchable access to patient data.

Source: ADB. 2020. Evaluation of Entrepreneurship Development Program in Indonesia. Final Report. TA 9678-INO: Advanced Knowledge and Skills for Sustainable Growth. Unpublished.

Table A5.2: Indonesian Tenants

Company/Team Leaders	Business Proposal	Internationalization	Comments
Code Laris TL: Meiga Satriya	The idea of an app store for selling and collecting e-books and courses that would maximize business growth. Profits in the range of Rp30 million per month	- This marketplace will target businesspeople in Europe, the US, and Indonesia - $86,000 to develop costs and advertising with a target of 2 years return	Minimum viable product (MVP)
PT Botika Teknologi Indonesia TL: Ditto Anindita	BOTIKA is an artificial intelligence company that focuses on natural language processing (NLP) and machine learning technology that fully understands Indonesian conversations.	Our technology also can be integrated into various social media channels such as LINE, WhatsApp, Facebook Messenger, Telegram, and Web Widget.	- No evidence of MVP - Technology based on digital application has potential to go international
Si Enis TL: Ali Alfian	E-helmet that can convert sunlight into electrical energy that can be directly used to charge a smartphone (original/unique feature)	Motorcycle rider is equal with helmet user (137.7 million in Indonesia). They are our general customers. But for European biker, we have other variants (power sport helmet and power hard hat).	- No evidence of MVP of the proposed products - Has a potential product for the European market

continued on next page

Table A5.2 continued

Company/Team Leaders	Business Proposal	Internationalization	Comments
Wi-Bat Felix Pasila	Part 1: Wireless battery offers an exclusive power bank with green issues in wireless transmission technology using graphene battery instead of lithium batteries—environment friendly	Part 2: Wireless battery is a conventional business that needs 3 consecutive years to break even. Market penetration will start from Indonesia, then Asian countries and finally Europe/US.	- No evidence of MVP - Not yet ready for European market—first step to go to other Asian countries
Varises Indonesia Niko Azhari Hidayat	One major health problem in Indonesia is low health awareness and limited access to health providers. Around 4.4 million adults in Indonesia will suffer from varicose veins. The web-based health information app Varises Indonesia uses a social impact multiplatform approach and cost-effectiveness principle.	Teleconsultation technology: We'll build an online and offline platform to provide online education training, referral, and comprehensive medical treatment. This progressive and elegant approach aims to build a network that enables patients to get high-quality medical care efficiently and increase medical providers' value. We plan for 5 years of funding with a 250 k/y burn rate to create better quality access to the community.	- No evidence of MVP: Online tools shows potential for internationalization
YONK Leonardus Gazali	YONK is unleashing the fishery potential with catalytic collaboration to finance the transition toward sustainable fisheries in Indonesia by removing the SILO with triple access to technology, financing, and market.		- No evidence of MVP: No insight for readiness to internationalization

k/y = kilo per year, SILO = single approach, US = United States.

Source: ADB. 2020. Evaluation of Entrepreneurship Development Program in Indonesia. Final Report. TA 9678-INO: Advanced Knowledge and Skills for Sustainable Growth. Unpublished.

Table A5.3: Mentors

	Name of Mentors/Location	Experience and Expertise	Role in AETP–SWISS Program
1	Wei Sun, Zurich	Intercultural management, supply chain management, and international cooperation	AETP training content
2	Meret Santos de Carvalho, Zurich	Operations and process, project management, marketing and event	Operations AETP
3	Lucky Esa, Jakarta	Innovation management, business model, product development, technology adoption	Mentor AETP
4	Kiwi Aliwarga, Jakarta	Organization design, strategic, operational	Mentor AETP
5	Virginie Verdon, Zurich	Nonexecutive boards or governance, financial management for or private and state, funding; state relations and international development, turnaround management	Partner BSTMC
6	Benedict Stalder, Zurich	Entrepreneurship education, coaching and mentoring, turnaround and acquisition integration management, business development and international sales, business model and tech	Partner BSTMC
7	Max Weber, Zurich	Innovation management, entrepreneurship and funding, global marketing, finance and economics, corporate strategy, international business, corporate boards, management and leadership	AETP program Manager, ZHAW SML

continued on next page

Table A5.3 continued

	Name of Mentors/Location	Experience and Expertise	Role in AETP–SWISS Program
8	Beat Walther, Zurich	Growth and innovation management, marketing and sales, entrepreneurship and corporate strategy, start-up coaching	Partner Vendbridge AG
9	Jacob Win, Jakarta	Digital business development, entrepreneurship, neurolinguistic programming, hypno copywriting, executive coaching, IT strategic planning, IT project management	AETP coach
10	RIKI Rijad, Indonesia	Strategic business— "creatigic" Integrated marketing and communication Digital marketing enthusiast Leadership in team management	Mentor AETP
11	Frank Silitonga, Indonesia	Sales and marketing, project management operational	Mentor AETP
12	Nicolas Berg, MSc Ec, Entrepreneur, Zurich	Entrepreneurship, disruptive start-ups: ICT, proptech, fintech, life sciences; start-up challenges: finance, funding, pitching, team; media relations, growth hacking, sales training	Trainer/coach start-up campus and venture lab
13	Ramona Lieser, Zurich	Innovation and entrepreneurship, social/impact entrepreneurship, content development, project management	AETP training content, ZHAW SML
14	Anna-Maria Strässner, Zurich	Communication and marketing, entrepreneurship, graphic design	AETP marketing, ZHAW SML
15	Angela Di Rosa, ZURICH	Leading across borders, business development, Southeast Asia	Senior consultant Southeast Asia
16	Fathoni Ahmad, EAST JAVA	Corporate strategy, finance and tax strategic planning, innovation management, business model, leadership	Mentor AETP
17	Risa Santoso, EAST JAVA	Business development, business model creation, training and education, people management, innovation and creativity	Mentor AETP
18	Alexander Epifanijanto, INDONESIA	Corporate strategy in Europe, international sales and marketing, innovation management, global brand strategy, leadership	Coordinator AETP, Indonesia
19	Ir. R. Eko Indrajit, JAKARTA	Government, consultant, business development and model creation, training and education, people management, innovation and creativity, information technology practices	Mentor AETP

AETP = Asia Entrepreneurship Training Program, ICT = information and communication technology, IT = information technology, SML = School of Management and Law, ZHAW = Zurich University of Applied Science.

Source: ADB. 2020. Evaluation of Entrepreneurship Development Program in Indonesia. Final Report. TA 9678-INO: Advanced Knowledge and Skills for Sustainable Growth. Unpublished.

www.ingramcontent.com/pod-product-compliance
Lightning Source LLC
Chambersburg PA
CBHW050056220326
41599CB00045B/7433